National Parks

GREAT SMOKY MOUNTAINS NATIONAL PARK

Trudy Becker

WWW.APEXEDITIONS.COM

Copyright © 2025 by Apex Editions, Mendota Heights, MN 55120. All rights reserved. No part of this book may be reproduced or utilized in any form or by any means without written permission from the publisher.

Apex is distributed by North Star Editions:
sales@northstareditions.com | 888-417-0195

Produced for Apex by Red Line Editorial.

Photographs ©: Shutterstock Images, cover, 1, 6–7, 12–13, 14–15, 16–17, 29, 32–33, 34–35, 36–37, 39, 42–43, 44–45, 46–47, 48–49; iStockphoto, 4–5, 8–9, 10–11, 40–41, 54–55, 56–57; Apic/Hulton Archive/Getty Images, 18–19; Picture History/Newscom, 20–21; Corbis Historical/Getty Images, 22–23; National Park Service, 24–25, 50–51, 58–59; Bettmann/Getty Images, 26–27; Mark A. Large/The Daily Times/AP Images, 30–31; Clay Owen/Knoxville News Sentinel/AP Images, 52–53; Red Line Editorial, 59

Library of Congress Control Number: 2024943072

ISBN
979-8-89250-455-3 (hardcover)
979-8-89250-471-3 (paperback)
979-8-89250-502-4 (ebook pdf)
979-8-89250-487-4 (hosted ebook)

Printed in the United States of America
Mankato, MN
012025

NOTE TO PARENTS AND EDUCATORS

Apex books are designed to build literacy skills in striving readers. Exciting, high-interest content attracts and holds readers' attention. The text is carefully leveled to allow students to achieve success quickly.

TABLE OF CONTENTS

Chapter 1
ENJOYING THE VIEW 4

Chapter 2
ALL ABOUT THE SMOKIES 8

Chapter 3
HISTORY 18

Natural Wonder
RAMSEY CASCADES 28

Chapter 4
HAVING FUN 30

Natural Wonder
KUWOHI 38

Chapter 5
WILDLIFE 41

Chapter 6
SAVING THE PARK 51

PARK MAP • 58
COMPREHENSION QUESTIONS • 60
GLOSSARY • 62
TO LEARN MORE • 63
ABOUT THE AUTHOR • 63
INDEX • 64

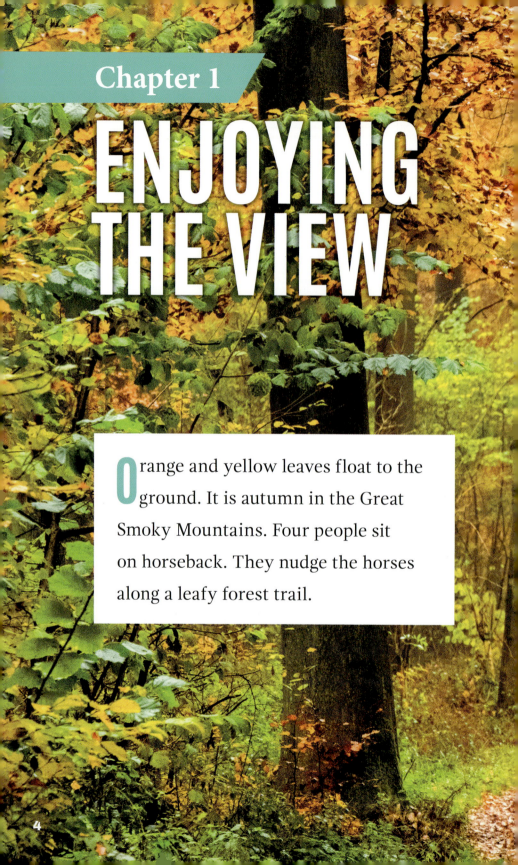

Chapter 1

ENJOYING THE VIEW

Orange and yellow leaves float to the ground. It is autumn in the Great Smoky Mountains. Four people sit on horseback. They nudge the horses along a leafy forest trail.

Guided horseback rides through the Smokies are available from March to November.

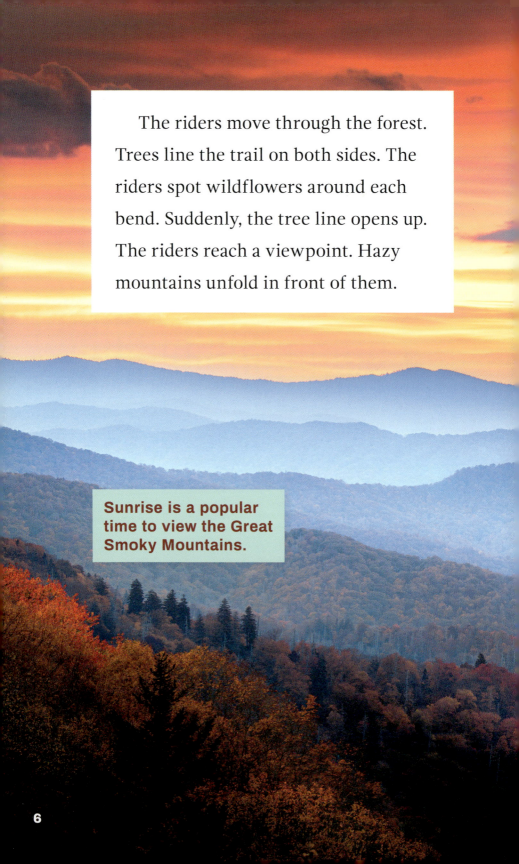

The riders move through the forest. Trees line the trail on both sides. The riders spot wildflowers around each bend. Suddenly, the tree line opens up. The riders reach a viewpoint. Hazy mountains unfold in front of them.

Sunrise is a popular time to view the Great Smoky Mountains.

THROUGH THE MOUNTAINS

Many people view the Great Smoky Mountains on foot. They hike trails in the park. Others drive on scenic roads. Some visitors even take carriages or hayrides.

Chapter 2

ALL ABOUT THE SMOKIES

Great Smoky Mountains National Park is located in two states. Part of the park is in Tennessee. The other part is in North Carolina. The land covers more than 500,000 acres (202,000 ha). The park is named for its main feature. The Great Smoky Mountains run through the whole park.

Millions of people visit the Smokies every year.

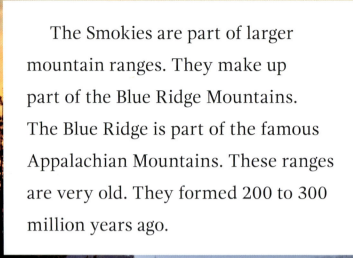

The Smokies are part of larger mountain ranges. They make up part of the Blue Ridge Mountains. The Blue Ridge is part of the famous Appalachian Mountains. These ranges are very old. They formed 200 to 300 million years ago.

FORMING THE MOUNTAINS

Shifting land created the Great Smoky Mountains. Plates of the earth slowly moved and crashed. That made new high and low points. Over time, land shifted even more. Its current shape is around one million years old.

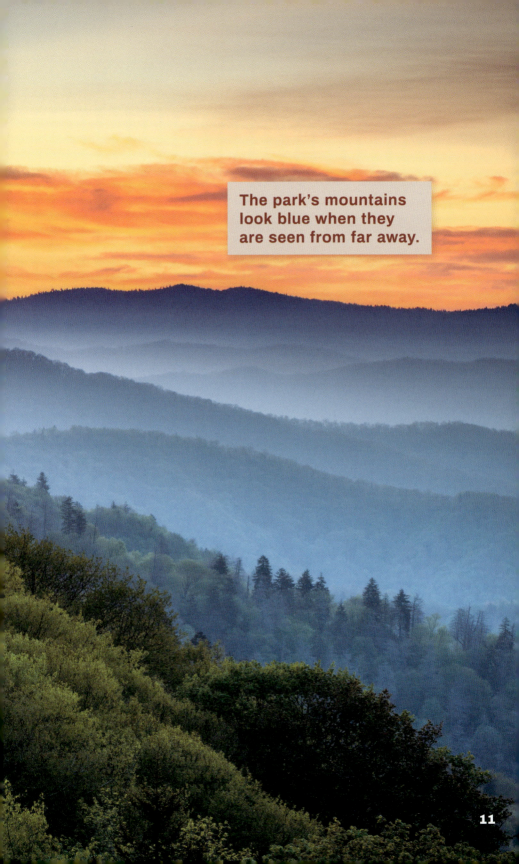

The park's mountains look blue when they are seen from far away.

Many visitors enjoy walking through the park's forests.

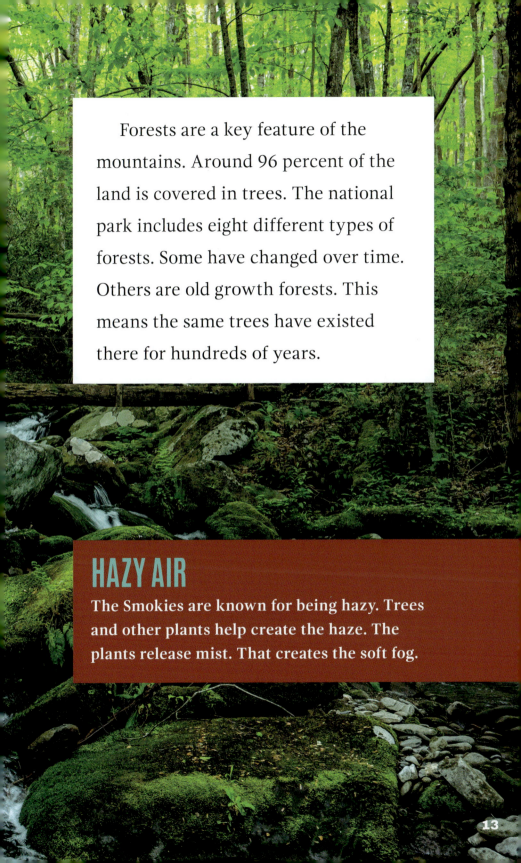

Forests are a key feature of the mountains. Around 96 percent of the land is covered in trees. The national park includes eight different types of forests. Some have changed over time. Others are old growth forests. This means the same trees have existed there for hundreds of years.

HAZY AIR

The Smokies are known for being hazy. Trees and other plants help create the haze. The plants release mist. That creates the soft fog.

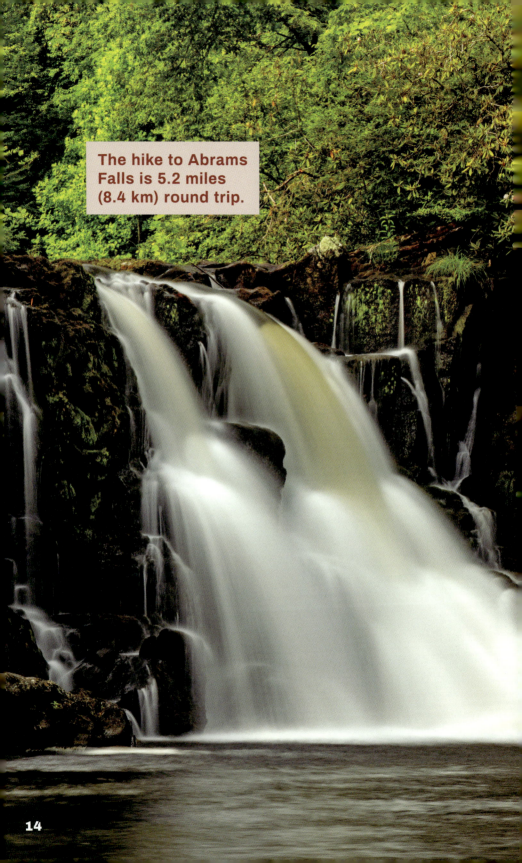
The hike to Abrams Falls is 5.2 miles (8.4 km) round trip.

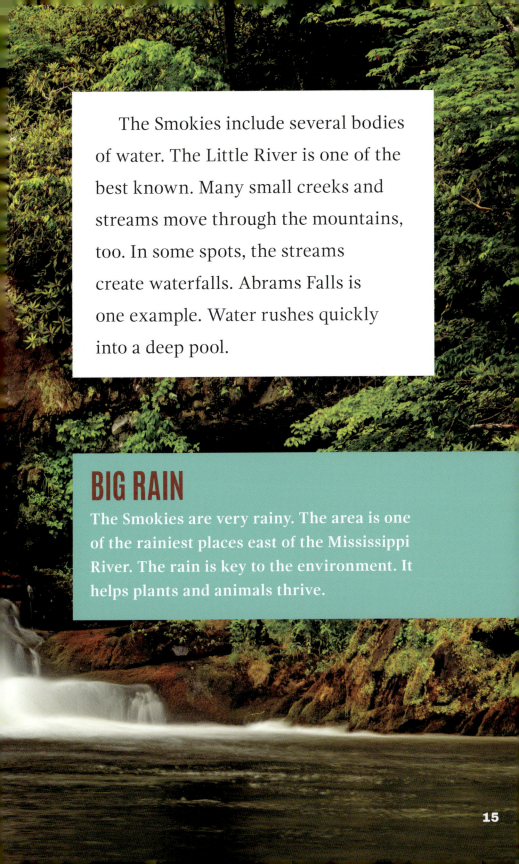

The Smokies include several bodies of water. The Little River is one of the best known. Many small creeks and streams move through the mountains, too. In some spots, the streams create waterfalls. Abrams Falls is one example. Water rushes quickly into a deep pool.

BIG RAIN

The Smokies are very rainy. The area is one of the rainiest places east of the Mississippi River. The rain is key to the environment. It helps plants and animals thrive.

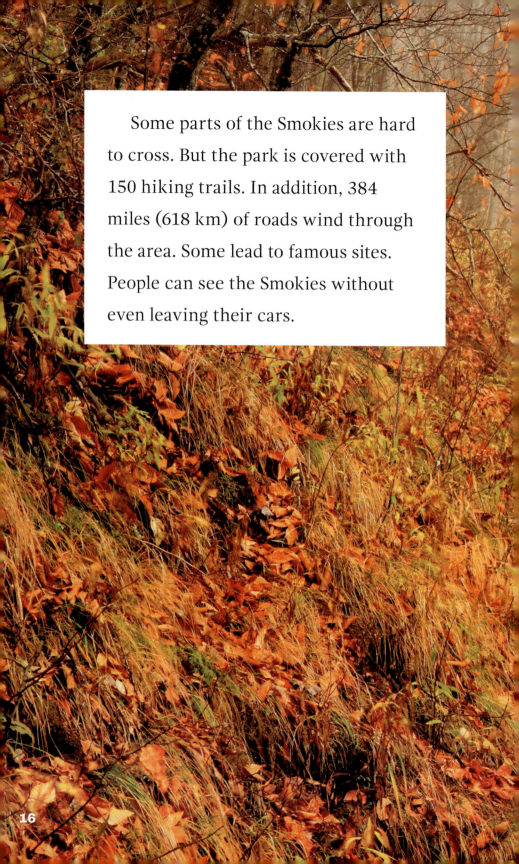

Some parts of the Smokies are hard to cross. But the park is covered with 150 hiking trails. In addition, 384 miles (618 km) of roads wind through the area. Some lead to famous sites. People can see the Smokies without even leaving their cars.

The park's trails cover about 850 miles (1,365 km).

Chapter 3
HISTORY

People have lived in the Smokies for thousands of years. The Cherokee people were early inhabitants. They hunted in the area. Families built small communities by the rivers. The Cherokee called the area *Shaconage*. That means "place of blue smoke."

Cherokee people get ready to play a ball game in the 1880s.

The US government forced the Cherokee to travel more than 1,000 miles (1,600 km) to what is now Oklahoma.

In the 1600s, European settlers began to arrive. They created conflicts. Settlers often fought with the Cherokee people. Over time, the settlers stole land. In 1830, the US government passed the Indian Removal Act. US soldiers forced the Cherokee people out of the Smokies. Thousands of Cherokees died on the journey. It was called the Trail of Tears.

OCONALUFTEE CHEROKEE

Some Cherokee were able to stay in their homeland. The Oconaluftee is one group. An Oconaluftee community still lives in the area today. They helped form the Eastern Band of Cherokee Indians. Their home is in North Carolina. It is close to the park's borders.

21

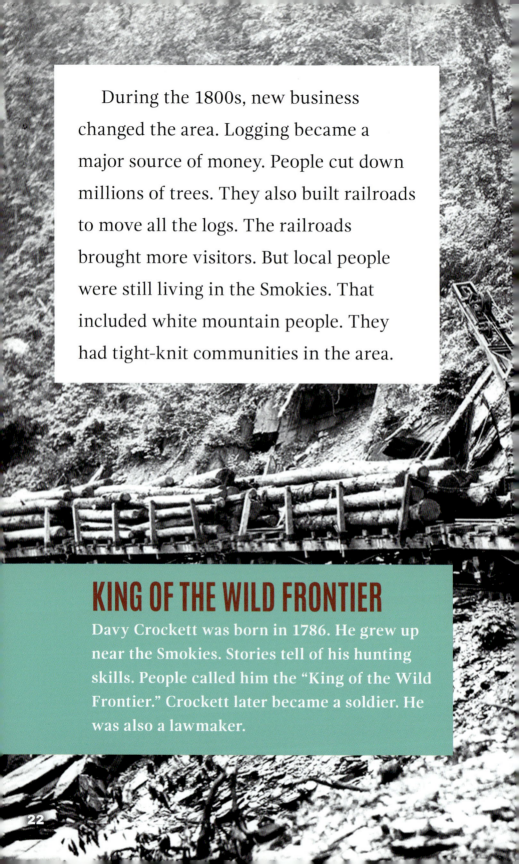

During the 1800s, new business changed the area. Logging became a major source of money. People cut down millions of trees. They also built railroads to move all the logs. The railroads brought more visitors. But local people were still living in the Smokies. That included white mountain people. They had tight-knit communities in the area.

KING OF THE WILD FRONTIER

Davy Crockett was born in 1786. He grew up near the Smokies. Stories tell of his hunting skills. People called him the "King of the Wild Frontier." Crockett later became a soldier. He was also a lawmaker.

A logging train rolls through the hills of Tennessee in the early 1900s.

By the 1900s, many people were worried about the land. They wanted it to stay wild. In 1926, their hopes came true. The area became a national park. The government bought land from mountain people. Tennessee and North Carolina both gave land, too. In the 1930s, workers prepared the area. They helped build trails.

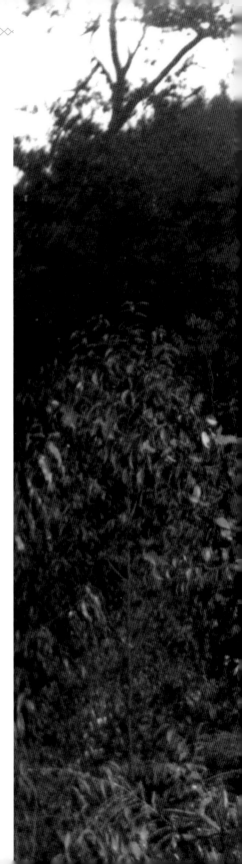

In the 1930s, government workers built trails all over the United States. The workers were part of the Civilian Conservation Corps.

The park finally opened in 1940. Over time, it grew and changed even more. People fixed old trails. They added new ones. They created welcome centers. Workers built roads, too. That way, more visitors could move through the park.

RACISM AT THE PARK

At first, park leaders wanted to keep Black and white people apart. No Black people were allowed to help build the park. Also, park leaders planned to have separate areas for Black people and white people. After 1950, that began to change. The park was open to all.

President Franklin D. Roosevelt speaks at the opening of Great Smoky Mountains National Park in 1940.

Natural Wonder
RAMSEY CASCADES

Ramsey Cascades is the park's tallest waterfall. It is also one of the most beautiful. Water rushes down 100 ft (30 m). It goes into a small pool of water. The area is full of rich wildlife. Salamanders live in the pool. Bears visit the area, too.

Reaching the waterfall is not easy. Visitors must hike 4 miles (6 km) on a rocky trail. Hikers move through old growth forests. Birch trees line the paths. In late spring, flowers bloom along the way.

The trail to Ramsey Cascades goes up nearly 2,200 feet (670 m).

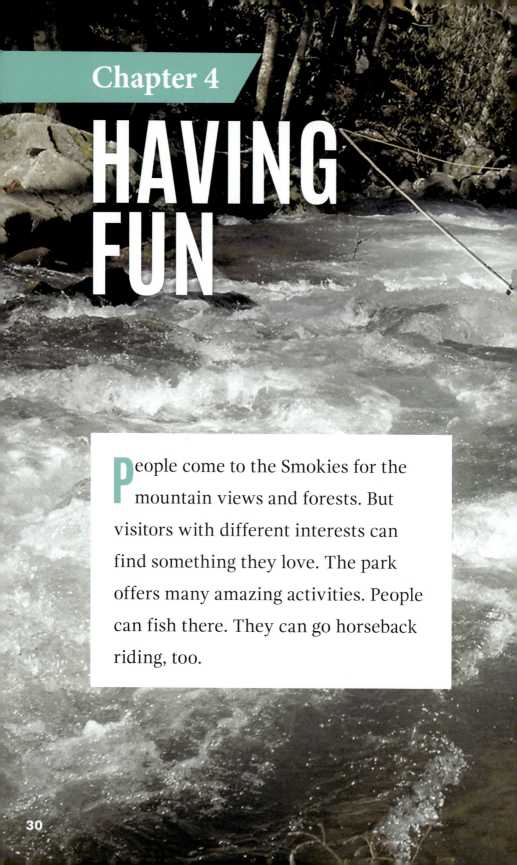

Chapter 4
HAVING FUN

People come to the Smokies for the mountain views and forests. But visitors with different interests can find something they love. The park offers many amazing activities. People can fish there. They can go horseback riding, too.

Fly fishing is a popular activity in the Great Smoky Mountains.

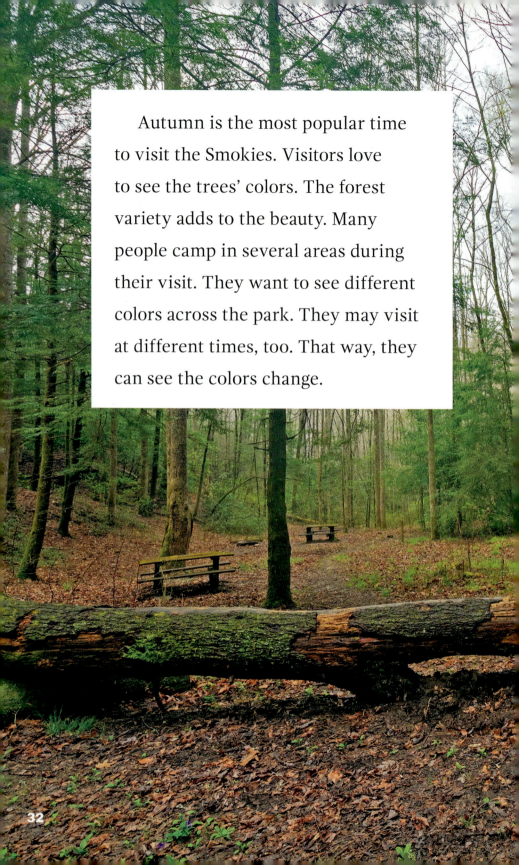

Autumn is the most popular time to visit the Smokies. Visitors love to see the trees' colors. The forest variety adds to the beauty. Many people camp in several areas during their visit. They want to see different colors across the park. They may visit at different times, too. That way, they can see the colors change.

The park has dozens of campsites where visitors can set up tents.

Some hiking trails offer incredible views of the mountains.

The park's hiking trails offer something for every visitor. Many trails are easy. They are great for beginners. Other trails are difficult. Alum Cave Trail is popular. It includes amazing views. Rocky Top is another popular spot. Visitors love its wildflowers. The Appalachian Trail also goes through the park.

APPALACHIAN TRAIL

The Appalachian Trail is very long. It covers 2,190 miles (3,525 km). The trail goes through eight states. It passes through six national parks, too. The part that goes through the Smokies is 72 miles (116 km) long.

Natural beauty is not the only park attraction. People also enjoy learning about the area's history. Cades Cove is a popular spot. It includes historic buildings. Many visitors drive through the area. They can see old churches and barns. It gives a picture of life in the past.

NEARBY FUN

Many visitors have fun outside the park, too. The theme park Dollywood is nearby. So is the Blue Ridge Parkway. This road features amazing views of the mountains. People drive to different points. They stop and admire the Blue Ridge.

Visitors can see an old building that used to be a school.

Natural Wonder

KUWOHI

Kuwohi is the highest point in the park. It is also the highest point of the Appalachian Trail. For many years, Kuwohi was known as Clingmans Dome. But in 2024, the park started using the mountain's Cherokee name.

Several trails lead to Kuwohi. A road also goes near it. A tower stands at the top of Kuwohi. It offers great views. Visitors can look across the mountains in all directions. On clear days, they can see for 100 miles (160 km). Many visitors go at sunrise or sunset. They enjoy the view when the light is changing.

The tower on Kuwohi was built in 1959.

Several kinds of owls live in the Great Smoky Mountains.

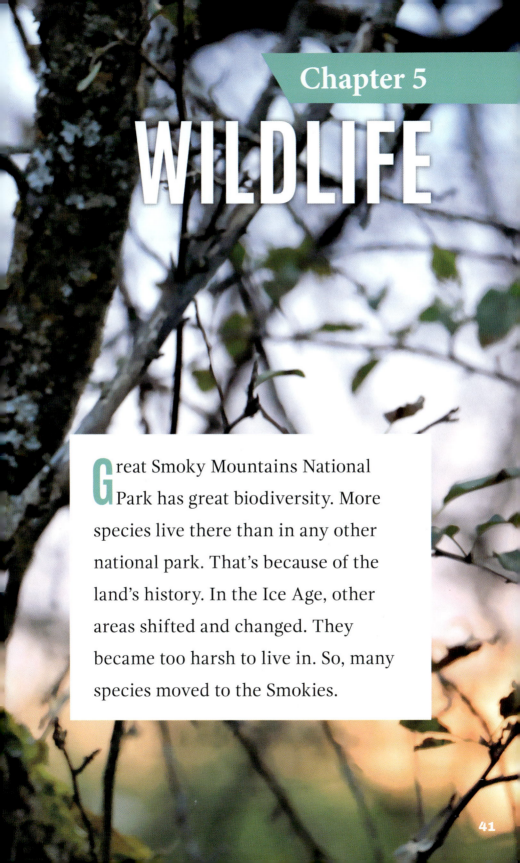

Chapter 5

WILDLIFE

Great Smoky Mountains National Park has great biodiversity. More species live there than in any other national park. That's because of the land's history. In the Ice Age, other areas shifted and changed. They became too harsh to live in. So, many species moved to the Smokies.

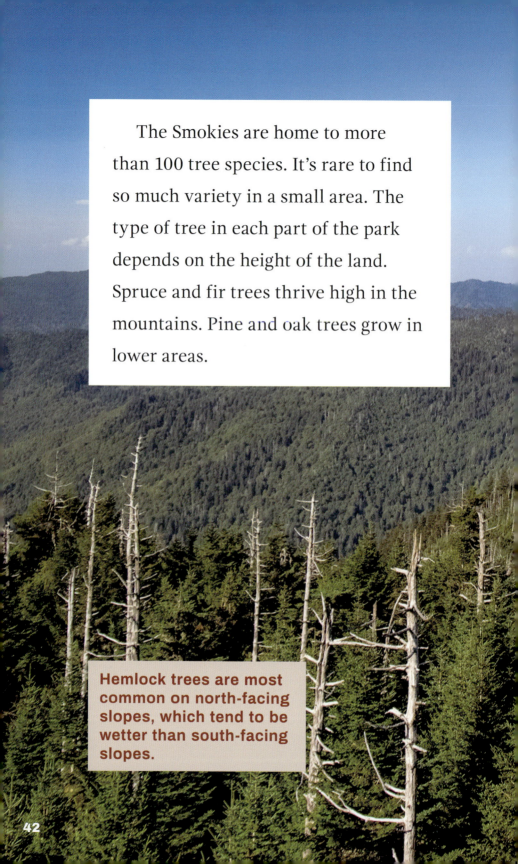

The Smokies are home to more than 100 tree species. It's rare to find so much variety in a small area. The type of tree in each part of the park depends on the height of the land. Spruce and fir trees thrive high in the mountains. Pine and oak trees grow in lower areas.

Hemlock trees are most common on north-facing slopes, which tend to be wetter than south-facing slopes.

LAND OF FLOWERS

The park includes 1,500 kinds of wildflower. Some people even call it Wildflower National Park. In high areas, rhododendrons bloom. The park includes two types of this flower. Visitors often look for mountain laurels, too.

Bears can be dangerous. Visitors should give them plenty of space.

The black bear is a symbol of the Smokies. Bears are the top predators in the area. They live all across the park. Visitors see bears most often near Cades Cove. Elk are another huge animal in the park. They can weigh up to 700 pounds (318 kg). Other common animals include deer and foxes.

ELK WATCH

Visitors love watching elk in the park. Some people make it an event. They sit and wait. They may even bring chairs and food. They often see many elk during their visit.

Many types of amphibians live in the Smokies. Some people call the park the "salamander capital of the world." The hellbender is one famous type. It is also known as the "snot otter." The hellbender is the park's longest salamander. It can grow to 30 inches (76 cm) long.

FISH HIGH AND LOW

The park includes many streams. Some are higher up. Others are low in the valleys. That means many different kinds of fish can survive. The brook trout is a native fish in the area.

Hellbenders breathe through their skin, so they need clean water.

Many kinds of butterflies can be seen in the Smokies.

The Smokies are full of fascinating insects. Beetles make their home in the forests. So do grasshoppers. Many visitors love the lightning bugs, also called fireflies. These bugs have back ends that glow. In May and June, they light up the night sky.

Workers study the park's plants and animals to make sure they stay healthy.

Chapter 6
SAVING THE PARK

Several parts of Great Smoky Mountains National Park face danger. Many of these problems are caused by people. Pollution harms native species. It hurts the land, too. Park officials hope to change that. They want to conserve the area.

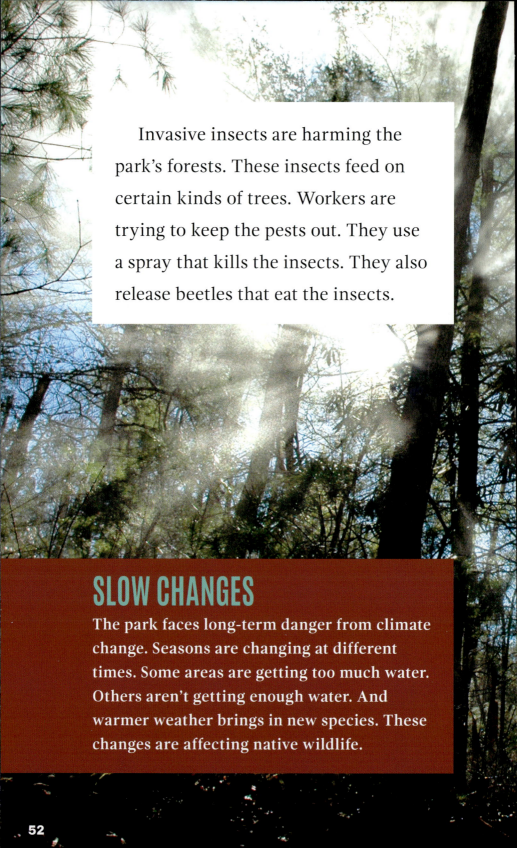

Invasive insects are harming the park's forests. These insects feed on certain kinds of trees. Workers are trying to keep the pests out. They use a spray that kills the insects. They also release beetles that eat the insects.

SLOW CHANGES

The park faces long-term danger from climate change. Seasons are changing at different times. Some areas are getting too much water. Others aren't getting enough water. And warmer weather brings in new species. These changes are affecting native wildlife.

A worker sprays hemlock trees to kill invasive insects.

Elk eat grasses, leaves, twigs, and shrubs.

Workers focus on other kinds of invasive species as well. For example, some invasive trout entered the park's waters. They started taking over the native fish. Workers try to remove the invasive fish so native fish can thrive.

The park helps native animals in many ways. In 2001, workers started bringing in more elk. The project was successful. Scientists are studying black bears, too. They want to learn how to keep the population up.

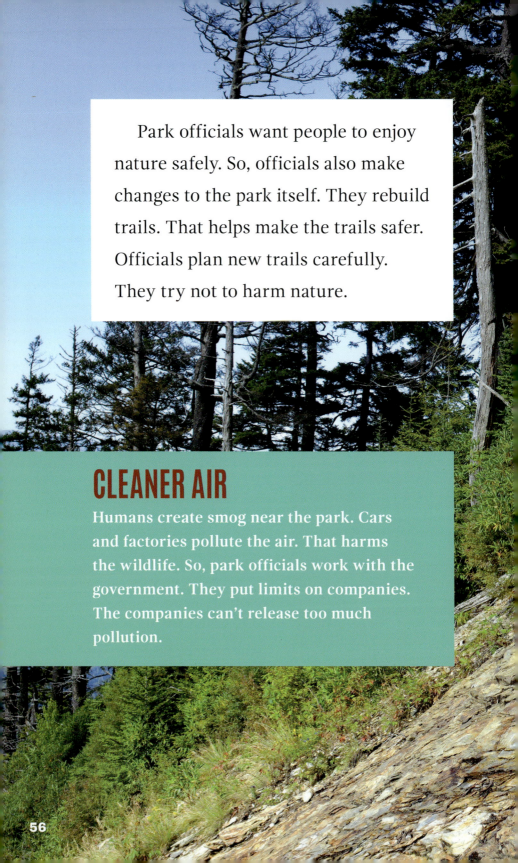

Park officials want people to enjoy nature safely. So, officials also make changes to the park itself. They rebuild trails. That helps make the trails safer. Officials plan new trails carefully. They try not to harm nature.

CLEANER AIR

Humans create smog near the park. Cars and factories pollute the air. That harms the wildlife. So, park officials work with the government. They put limits on companies. The companies can't release too much pollution.

It's important to stay on trails when hiking. That way, other parts of the park will stay healthy.

PARK MAP

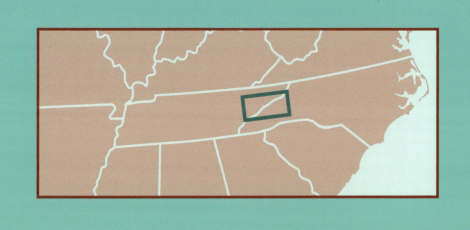

COMPREHENSION QUESTIONS

Write your answers on a separate piece of paper.

1. Write a few sentences describing the different kinds of wildlife found in Great Smoky Mountains National Park.

2. If you were going to visit Great Smoky Mountains National Park, what would you be most interested in seeing? Why?

3. When did Great Smoky Mountains National Park open?
   - A. 1830
   - B. 1926
   - C. 1940

4. How might beetles help the park's forests?
   - A. They could eat invasive insects.
   - B. They could eat the park's trees.
   - C. They could eat large salamanders.

5. What does **conflicts** mean in this book?

*In the 1600s, European settlers began to arrive. They created **conflicts**. Settlers often fought with the Cherokee people.*

- A. friendly events
- B. food and water
- C. problems

6. What does **conserve** mean in this book?

*Pollution harms native species. It hurts the land, too. Park officials hope to change that. They want to **conserve** the area.*

- A. hurt
- B. keep safe
- C. cut down

Answer key on page 64.

GLOSSARY

biodiversity
The number of different species that live in an area.

climate change
A dangerous long-term change in Earth's temperature and weather patterns.

frontier
A wild area not settled by humans.

hazy
Foggy and not clear.

inhabitants
People who live in an area.

invasive
Spreading quickly in a new area and causing many problems there.

native
Originally living in an area.

scenic
Having views of beautiful nature.

species
Groups of animals or plants that are similar and can breed with one another.

symbol
An object or idea that stands for and reminds people of something else.

TO LEARN MORE

BOOKS

Bowman, Chris. *Great Smoky Mountains National Park*. Minneapolis: Bellwether Media, 2023.

Bright, Annie. *Tennessee*. Minneapolis: Abdo Publishing, 2023.

Lassieur, Allison. *The National Parks Encyclopedia*. Minneapolis: Abdo Publishing, 2023.

ONLINE RESOURCES

Visit **www.apexeditions.com** to find links and resources related to this title.

ABOUT THE AUTHOR

Trudy Becker lives in Minneapolis, Minnesota. She likes exploring new places and loves anything involving books.

INDEX

Abrams Falls, 15
Appalachian Mountains, 10
Appalachian Trail, 35, 36

bears, 28, 45, 55
Blue Ridge Mountains, 10, 36

Cades Cove, 36, 45
camping, 32
Cherokee, 18, 21
climate change, 52
conservation, 51–52, 55–56
Crockett, Davy, 22

elk, 45, 55

fishing, 30
forests, 4, 6, 13, 28, 30, 32, 42, 49, 52

hiking, 7, 16, 28, 35
horseback riding, 4, 6, 30

insects, 49, 52
invasive species, 52, 55

Kuwohi, 38

logging, 22

Oconaluftee, 21

pollution, 51, 56

racism, 27
railroads, 22
Ramsey Cascades, 28
roads, 7, 16, 26, 36, 38

salamanders, 28, 46

Trail of Tears, 21
trails, 4, 6–7, 16, 24, 26, 28, 35, 38, 56

wildflowers, 6, 28, 35, 43

ANSWER KEY:
1. Answers will vary; 2. Answers will vary; 3. C; 4. A; 5. C; 6. B